HOW DEALS

ARE DONE

A Guide to

Quick Sales

Forest Ivey

ISBN 978-0-692-07376-6

Garamond font

Forest Ivey is available for readings and seminars.

tsutamorisan@gmail.com

To my wife, Kathleen,

for empowering me to be the best I can be.

About the Author

First and foremost, I'm a teacher. I found my way into the world of sales inadvertently. My original aim was to become a foreign language instructor. With an undergrad in psychology I found it impossible to acquire a profession in my desired field. Despite having lived in Germany as an exchange student and having lived in Japan as an English instructor, I could not find a position teaching foreign languages in America without the relative prerequisites.

While pursing my graduate degree in linguistics, I took a part time job in timeshare marketing with Silverleaf Resorts. I quickly realized the monetary potential that sales had to offer, and I allowed that position to be the engine of growth that payed for my schooling. Once I acquired my graduate degree, I was offered a management position in timeshare marketing. A choice had to be made: continue on the path to academia or stick to sales. The answer was clear.

Having combined my sense for teaching along with my sense for sales, I found my true calling. My teams of marketing salespeople annually set sales records. If anyone can combine years of sales experience into a compacted course, then I have truly provided it for you. Rest assured that the direction I offer is the same direction I have offered to many up and coming sales-people. Years and years of successful sales training has fine-tuned my process. Allow me to show you how deals are done and you will be closing deals in no time.

Forest Ivey 2018

Table of Contents

How Deals Are Done

Introduction

Once mastered, sales is a creative and highly rewarding skill that can be both monetarily beneficial and effective in personal, day to day interactions. This book is meant to be an easy reference for the development of proven sales tactics. Many of the tactics in this book are based on simple psychology; the advantage is being able to predict what people will say and do in certain situations.

The tactics outlined in this book were developed from my experience as an OPC agent. OPC stands for "Off Property Contact," which is the most commonly used term to describe timeshare marketing agents. The job of an OPC agent is to talk to hundreds of people each week and convince them to commit to a date and time for a timeshare presentation. Given the negative stigma associated with the timeshare industry, one can imagine the uphill battle that every OPC agent faces in the field. That being said, rest assured that the tactics presented in this book are tried and true.

The time allowed for an OPC agent to make a sale is very short – typically, only one or two minutes is all that's available. People with sales backgrounds of many kinds have tried the role of OPC agent thinking that it would be just like selling cars, clothes, houses, etc. The truth of the matter is that quick sales and long sales are very different, but quick sales tactics can still be applied to long sales, too. Lucky for you, no matter what type of sales skills you are seeking to strengthen, this book will benefit you.

Each chapter of this book stands on its own and can be practiced separately from the others. The chapters are short and to the point; they are meant to be easily understood and *practiced*. Don't take pride in finishing this book in a day; instead, take pride in putting each chapter to use. After all, reading a book on how to play piano isn't nearly as effective as actually *practicing* playing the piano. The same holds true for developing sales skills. Simple things are powerful and powerful things are simple. This book is both simple and powerful.

Chapter 1 / The Warmup

No one wants to be sold anything, but everyone wants to buy things.

Take a minute to think about that sentence. Imagine you are going shopping for a new TV. You enter the store, head for the TV section, and start studying the screens and prices. Someone approaches you and says, "Sir, are you looking for anything in particular today?".

Naturally, you give the exact same response as everyone else: "I'm just looking." No need to let that guy bother you. After all, he probably gets a percentage of whatever you decide you buy. He'll probably just push some product on you that's in his best interest.

Now imagine that same salesperson approaches you and instead says something completely unrelated to work – something like, "Did you see the latest episode of [whatever]?".

Whether you've seen the show he mentioned or not, suddenly you are having a conversation with the guy about one topic and the next. One TV show leads to another, the topic of TV shows then leads to other interests, and before you know it you are talking about where you grew up, what your hobbies are, and what you do for a living.

Essentially, you've just been "warmed up." Now you are in the right state of mind to trust the salesperson, who, after all, is clearly interested in who you are and what you have to say. This guy is more interested in helping you find the right TV instead of just selling you something. He's just a person. He's not a salesperson. Eventually the conversation will transition back to the topic of looking for the right TV set.

There are many ways to get your warmup started. Be creative! If the suggestions here don't sound like things you would normally say, then by all means think of some of your own. Warmups can begin with anything from the mundane, ranging all the way to the utterly absurd. For example, you might simply ask "Do you know what time it is?", or you might say something along the lines of "There's a guy out there in the parking lot wearing a clown suit and passing out sandals! Have you seen him?".

Honestly, saying anything that is *not* work related is the right thing to say. If your first impression screams "I'm a salesperson!" then you will be fighting an uphill battle.

One good way to find specific topics with which to begin conversations would be by observing people's clothing. If someone is wearing a pair of shoes that you like, then you might ask them where they bought them. If someone is wearing a shirt with the name of a band on it, then you might ask what their favorite song is from that band. If someone is wearing a jersey or any other clothing with a team's logo, then that gives you another easy opening for conversation.

Challenging loyalties is a fantastic way of getting conversations started. If someone is wearing their favorite team's jersey, you might question that team's ability or even question that person's loyalty to their team. If someone is wearing a hat displaying a brand-name for a car, then ask them if *all* their cars are of that brand or if it is just a hat they are wearing. When people are proud of brands, they will defend them and tell you why; if you just agree with their choice of brand, then the conversation will be a lot shorter.

Although it may seem counter-intuitive at first, disagreeing with someone shows them that you are being yourself and that you are not just attempting to agree in order to get close. There is a time to agree and a time to disagree. During the warmup is the only time it is okay to disagree. Remember this for later.

"Warming up the customer" is an easy, relaxed process that causes the potential customer to drop their shields, leaving them open for a sale. But it also gives you a chance to do some fact-finding with the customer in order to find out what kind of product they'd be interested in. If the customer is looking for a TV, for instance, you already know that they are there for that type of product, but what you don't know is: which one or for whom it is being purchased, or where it will be going, or even if they are interested in buying today at all. If the customer mentions that they live in a town over two hours away from your store, then you might ask what they are doing in town – perhaps they have family or some event they're attending. If the customer replies they do not have family in town, but rather that they come in town once a month to shop, then you can bet they are motivated buyers!

If you're selling cars and you discover that the customer has three children and the husband drives a sports car, then you can logically start to narrow down the choices you will be offering them - minivans and SUVs come to mind. If they mention they are loyal to a particular brand, then your job is only getting easier before you even get around to talking business. Think of the small talk in the warmup as reconnaissance – information gathering. Once you gather enough information you can focus your efforts on offering the customer something that is unique to their needs before you even find out what their needs are. For example, if you're selling someone a house, finding out as much about their lives as possible can only benefit how you talk to them about certain properties. Car guys might want nice garages without steep driveways. Big families might want multiple bathrooms. Entertainers might want large patios or dining areas. You get the idea. Obviously, there exist a multitude of products to sell; however, understanding what the customer wants before they even tell you can be a powerful tool that the customer will only understand as empathy.

In short, the warmup is the foundation upon which your 30-second relationship is built, and it is also where you gather facts pertaining to the customer in order to better sculpt your sales-pitch in relation to their needs. Once a relationship is established, you can begin to transition into the rest of your routine. If the customer's shields are not dropped within the first 30 seconds of speaking with them, then keep going - some people are more skeptical than others.

The concept of **rhythm** is important to every step of the sales process and will be mentioned throughout this book. Your rhythm is key! When sales take place in a short amount of time, one must be very conscious of rhythm. Keep in mind that the pace you set during your warmup will establish the rhythm for the remainder of your routine. When it comes to short sales, you must play the role of the drummer and the customer must dance to your beat. You are in control and you guide the turns the conversation takes.

Regarding rhythm, each customer will react differently to a faster or slower pace. So how do you know what tempo to use? It's simple.

Be the customer...plus 1!

If the customer is slow, be "slow plus 1." If the customer is fast, be "fast plus 1." Mirror the customer, but always be a little bit quicker. Doing so allows the customer to identify with you while you retain the ability to guide the conversation. To call upon exaggerations, a sleepy person would not last 30 seconds in a conversation with someone who just downed 3 espressos. Similarly, the espresso drinker would be uninterested in the drooling-on of someone as slow paced as the sleepy person. Match the customer, but guide them. Be sensitive to your audience!

If you find that you are naturally a slow-paced person, then do your best to imitate someone you can think of that speaks more quickly. Even if you can't exactly match the speech-speed of your fast-paced person, at least you will increase your *own* speed. The opposite is true of naturally fast-paced people as well. If you naturally speak in a fast-paced manner and you are out-talking your customers, then do your best to impersonate someone who is extremely slow-paced. Once again, you will find that your imitation may not hit the mark, but your rhythm will land somewhere in between and will be closer to the pace you are looking for. Once you become more sensitive to pacing yourself slightly ahead of your customer, you will find that you can guide them through the sales process more gracefully.

Be a person, not a salesperson. Ask about the customer and let them talk. Do some fact-finding and some friend-making. This doesn't mean being over-flattering. Instead, challenge them. Be sensitive of your pace in relation to theirs, and always stay one step ahead. This is how to cultivate the right environment for sales. This is how deals are done.

How Deals Are Done

Chapter 2 / The Tiedown

The "tiedown" is essentially the act of getting the customer to agree to wanting something you are selling. It is much easier to *hypothetically* agree to buy something when money is not actually involved. Therefore, if the customer agrees with your hypothetical question, it establishes two things: value in your product and an opening for your pitch. Once the customer hypothetically agrees to wanting your product, then they have no good reason not to listen to your pitch.

Tiedowns are typically structured in the "if-then" format. For example,

"If you could find a TV in your price range, then you would buy one, right?"

Or perhaps something like this:

"If you could find a TV you like, you would buy one today, right?"

Notice that these are actually statements turned into questions. Subconsciously you're telling the customer what to do and then adding the word "right?" on the end. It's very simple to do. You love this book, right? You are going to recommend it to your friends, right? See how it easy it is!

In the world of sales, yes/no questions are usually avoided unless the answer is obviously "Yes". Offering the option to say "No" gives the customer an out that you do not need to provide. In other words, if for any reason you plan to ask the customer a yes/no question (such as the examples above), ask them in a way such that they are actually **commands** turned into **questions**.

Tiedowns must not only be "one-liners" either. Sometimes it's more fitting to narrow down their choices within your tiedown in order to establish the customer's exact needs. A three-part tiedown caters to the customer better and also makes it easier for you as a salesperson to put the customer in front of a product they actually want. A three-part tiedown would sound something like this:

(1) "What room are you looking to put a TV in?"

(2) "Which brands did you have in mind?"

(3) "If we could find a TV under your price range, you would buy one today, right?"

Assuming the customer answered "yes" to your tiedown, they are now all ears for whatever you are going to pitch. The customer told you what they want and told you they will buy. Time to put something in front of them!

How Deals Are Done

If the customer answers "no" to your tiedown, do not worry. Not everyone you talk to will be interested in buying. You should assume that everyone wants to buy from you; however, if someone cannot afford what you are selling or is just simply not interested then use your time wisely and go on to the next available prospect. The tiedown functions as a hook for those who are actually interested and functions as a screening for those who are not. If someone cannot afford a Ferrari, don't try to sell them one. But never assume they cannot buy, investigate first. Do a little warming up and tying down. If they fall in place, then it is time to pitch!

Regarding your rhythm, the transition from your warmup into your tiedown should be seamless. In other words, the customer should not notice once you guide the conversation back in the direction of sales. One minute you are talking about TV shows, then internet providers, then family life, then hobbies, and then what room needs a TV. Since you are matching the customer's speed +1, you have the position to guide the conversation quite effortlessly. It may look something like this:

Salesperson: Did you see the latest episode of [whatever] last night?

Customer: No, I don't watch that show, but my son watches it.

Salesperson: You should definitely check it out sometime! How many kiddos are in the family?

Customer: Just two.

Salesperson: How old are they?

Customer: They're 12 and 15, both boys.

Salesperson: Do they play any sports?

Customer: They're into baseball mostly, but they play soccer, too.

Salesperson: Have you taken them to see a ball game or do you just watch them on TV?

Customer: Yeah, I've taken them to a couple games, but we usually just watch from home.

Salesperson: What room were you looking to put a TV in?

Customer: I want to put one in the kitchen, so I can watch something while the kids watch the big TV.

Salesperson: Which brands did you have in mind?

Customer: I was thinking [whatever].

Salesperson: If you could find a TV under your price range, you would buy one today, right?

Customer: Well, yeah, of course.

The last question in your tiedown should be such a no-brainer that "of course" is the only appropriate response. Also, the transition from warmup to tie-down is smoothest if you can guide the warmup material somewhat in the direction of the product you are selling. In the example above, the question was asked if the customer watches the ball games on TV, after which the customer was asked for which room the TV was needed. The space in between these two lines is where the warmup ended and the tiedown began, but the customer would never be aware of this.

As long as your rhythm is one step ahead of the customer's rhythm then leading them through emotional topics should be a breeze. For some people this comes naturally, but for others it may take some practice. People love to talk about themselves, so let them. Once they are emotionally charged from talking about their own lives, they are ripe for a tiedown. And once they agree to the tiedown, they are ripe for a pitch.

You wouldn't go out on a first date and move in for a kiss upon meeting someone at their door, would you? Timing is everything! First comes the small talk, then establish their values, then go for the gold. This is how deals are done.

How Deals Are Done

Chapter 3 / The Pitch

Strategically present the details of your product. The sooner your pitch is memorized, the sooner you will make money. It is most likely the case that the product you're selling already has a pitch. My advice to you is to follow that pitch! Memorize it well! After all, people before you have written and used many pitches, and if there was a better pitch for you to learn, then you would be better off learning *that* pitch. Do not give up on the pitch you were taught simply because you have not been successful with it yet. Everything takes fine tuning. Memorizing your pitch is just the first step before you can actually get anywhere close to selling. Think of it like this: memorizing the pitch is the equivalent of putting strings on a guitar. Just stringing the guitar will not get you anywhere unless you learn how to tune it. The songs you play will not sound good unless you can tune your guitar, and you cannot tune your guitar unless you learn to string it first.

Chances are, if you are reading this book, memorizing your pitch is not something that you need help in accomplishing. If you are seeking help in memorization techniques, however, then I would do every single one of the following suggestions:

- Write your pitch down over and again.

- Pitch your friends and family members.

- Pitch to yourself in a mirror.

- Record yourself reading the pitch.

Work on one line at a time before moving on to the next. Remember, good practice creates good habits. Patience is key when memorizing your pitch. If you routinely practice mistakes then your mistakes will become memorized. If you think it takes reading, writing, and recording your pitch 10 times in order to memorize it, then read and write and record it 30 times instead. You have the time.

Perfecting your pitch is an investment in yourself. The sooner you learn your pitch, the sooner you can begin to make money. And isn't that the whole point? If you are currently working in a sales position and you are reading this book then you're probably searching for how to improve your closing ratio. Ask yourself first if you even have the original pitch memorized. If the answer is no, then stop what you are doing and just go memorize your pitch already. There is no short cut for hard work! If you do know the pitch you were taught but you are not closing your target number of deals, ask yourself if you're actually using the original pitch? Take a moment and write out your pitch; is it what you were taught or is it something else? Sometimes a bit of self-reflection will tell you if you've changed the original pitch into something else.

It is possible for you to develop a pitch rather than to follow one. If you are in a leadership position and this applies to you, here are some simple guidelines to follow when designing a pitch. The basic structure is not complicated:

(1) describe the product, then

(2) mention some perks, then

(3) mention its best parts.

It is similar to the pattern of good / better / best, but instead, it is more along the lines of: basic / great / amazing. When you've told the customer the amazing part, it will be time to close.

Think about the structure of an infomercial and you should get the idea. We are all familiar with the infomercials on TV describing some product that is seemingly uninteresting until suddenly you are drawn in and curious to learn more. Infomercials can take anywhere from 5 to 30 minutes, but that much time is not available for someone practicing quick sales. If you have left some information out of your pitch, then that leaves the customer asking questions about your product. If they're asking questions about your product, then that just means that they're interested in buying! Plus, you are probably aware of what questions they will ask next since your pitch only discloses so much. Being able to quickly answer their predictable questions only makes you look more knowledge-able and trustworthy about the product.

So what information should you include in your pitch? It's simple. Essentially, your pitch should be an emotional ladder. Always lead the customer toward what they want. Introduce the product, describe its good points, and then hit them with something so nice about it that they are truly taken aback. That's it.

Simplicity is the key when showing your product. Naturally, the customer will want what you are show-ing them. The tiedown will have already established their interest. Now show them the benefits of moving one step further toward what they want. If they are hesitant, that is normal. Be confident. Be relaxed. Be patient. Let them ask you questions.

A lesson in pitching a product would be incomplete without the mention of the role of **rhythm**. Once again, rhythm can make or break your delivery of the information. Rhythm and simplicity can be combined to create a very powerful pitch indeed. Einstein once said,

"If you can't explain it to a 6-year-old, you don't understand it yourself."

Think about that quote. How would you explain something to a 6-year-old that would allow them to go forth and explain what you just told them to others? How could you describe something so plainly that anyone could understand? Be wary of having your pitch so well memorized that the information seems to spew out at a fast pace. If you pitch too quickly, you might lose the customer's attention right off the bat. If the information you feed them is simple and amazing, then it will be swallowed swiftly. If that information is paced acceptably, then each bit will sink in.

Pay as much attention to the information in the pitch as you do to the pauses between each line. Think of each line of your pitch as a spoonful of ice cream you are feeding the customer. You don't want to feed them too quickly or they won't be able to appreciate each bite. Not only that, but they won't be able to taste the many flavors you are feeding them.

Imagine you are about to pitch a husband and wife, but just before you start to pitch, the wife is distracted by one of their children. You are left with only the husband to hear you. Your pitch must be so simple and rhythmic and amazing that the husband could quite easily turn to his wife, once back from tending to their child, and deliver all the necessary information to pitch his wife by himself. Thinking requires effort, so don't force the customer to think about the pitch. Just deliver the goods. Do not give in to the temptation to over-explain your product. Too much information will only confuse the customer and give them an out. If the customer wants to buy, they will buy. If the customer wants to ask questions first, they will buy. This is how deals are done.

How Deals Are Done

Chapter 4 / Closing the Deal

Ask for the commitment, ask for the money. Ask and ye shall receive. If you are new to sales then, closing deals might make you nervous. Rookie salesmen see closing as a disturbance to the customer. After all, if a customer wants to buy something, then they will speak up and pay for it, right? Why should you have to ask for payment? In this day and age, becoming a face to face salesperson, a real salesperson, is becoming a lost art. So much so that when jobs are created that require "real salesmen" they are hard to find! And if, by chance, you are hired to fill those shoes, you might feel uncomfortable closing the sale. Think about it, the last 100 things you bought were probably either online or required no salesperson in the first place.

Do not be afraid to ask someone for money! If this is a hurdle for you, then welcome the growing pain. If you're not paining, then you're not gaining. Get out of your comfort zone and enjoy getting a good paycheck. Think of these circumstances as your opportunity. This is your opportunity to do something that most people cannot do! This is your opportunity to provide a service that most people cannot provide! That is called job security.

How Deals Are Done

If you are new to sales, then first things first: *always assume the answer is yes*. Would <u>you</u> buy what you are selling? If the answer is no, then your thoughts, actions, intentions, inflections, and body language will all say the same thing. If you know what you are selling is a quality product, then life is easy! Simply get your product in front of as many people as necessary and assume that everyone wants to buy it. Once your routine is so well memorized that it requires little to no thought, then I suggest the only thought in your mind should be the word "yes" repeated over and again. Repeat the word "yes" so rapidly that if one could hear your thoughts, they would assume you are crazy. Become overwhelmed with the word 'yes' and so will everyone around you. Everyone wants what you are selling. That should be obvious.

Yes yes yes yes yes yes yes yes yes yes yes yes yes...

All pitches end by asking the customer for payment, so how should you do that? Essentially, you should give the customer two options: (1) buy it this way or (2) buy it that way. In the sales world, this technique is known as a "choice close."

Since you have already assumed the customer wants what you are selling, the only real question should be how they intend to take the product home. Always offer the customer options. After all, it is their choice that they buy. You are not selling, they are simply buying.

For example, 'choice closes' might sound like any of the following:

- "Will that be debit or credit?"

- "Who has better handwriting?"

- "Are you right handed or left handed?"

- "Will you be paying in full or finance?"

- "Will that be ten or twenty percent down?"

- "Will you pick up today or tomorrow?"

- "Would you like pick up or delivery?"

- "Will we be shipping to billing or home?"

- "Do you want sports or eco package?"

- "Do you want the silver or the grey one?"

You get the idea. Always give the customer the freedom to choose, as long as both options are to pay you.

The same goes for giving options throughout your pitch. Instead of offering "yes vs. no," only offer choices that lead toward the close. For example, if you ask the customer in the middle of your pitch something along the lines of "Does that sound great to you?", the customer has an option to leave. Imagine this: you are describing your product to a customer and, before you get to the best part, you ask the customer "yes or no" about what they have heard so far. This is a terrible habit that many salesmen fall into! If you've been a salesperson for years but cannot figure out why you are not closing, then perhaps making this one change is all that you need to employ. Think of it like this: no one would ask you what you think of a movie if you have not yet finished it, so why would you ask the customer if they like what you have shown them if you haven't finished your routine?

Keep your closing line as short as possible. The customer should not realize that they were just presented with an option. Instead, they should just react emotionally to the options you've given them. If your close is simple and straight forward, then the customer will respond accordingly. If your closing line is longer than 10 syllables, then it is time to get a new line. Take a look once more at the closing lines previously offered and study how they've been simplified. If your closing line is this simple, then the customer will not feel as though they were presented with a choice. It will instead seem natural. Remember, there is power in simplicity. What is powerful is simple and what is simple is powerful. Although you are reading a book on how to be a salesperson, presenting yourself as if you are not a salesperson is half the trick. Be relaxed, be fun, be simple. Treat your customers with respect, but don't try to be too professional. When finalizing a deal, keep your closing line nice and neat.

This is where it gets really interesting. Sometimes the best closing line is not having one at all. Talk about simple! The "assumed" close is very powerful and can really streamline the closing process. Imagine you have just finished your routine and, instead of asking for the close, you just ask the customer to hold a pen and start filling out the paperwork. Assuming the customer is ready to buy requires some intuition of the customer's reactions to your pitch. If you've created a good relationship with them and they've been involved with your pitch, then the best course of action may be to simply assume they are buying your product. With the example of the TV salesperson, for instance, you would simply order the product to be taken to checkout on behalf of the customer and you would give him a handshake and tell him it is waiting for him at the register. Since you're on a roll, continue to ask if there are any other accessories for the new TV the customer may want to look at today. He might say yes!

Once again, the role of rhythm finalizes each deal. Do not allow any downtime for the customer to regret the choices they've made. Instead, reward the customer's choices by keeping them emotionally involved. Keeping the customer in an emotional state of mind is very easy: continue to ask the customer about emotional topics. Even though there will probably be a point at which the customer can think twice about what they are doing, you should not allow this time to be filled with buyer's remorse. So, continue with warmup material even though you are much later in your routine.

For example, imagine for a moment that you have just convinced the customer to buy a certain TV, car, or phone, etc. What comes next? Paperwork and logic come next. Perhaps you walk the customer to some area where they can sign papers and pay up. Do you allow this time to be filled with silence? No! Do you allow the customer to second guess the fact that they must now fork over the money? No way! Continue your emotional warm up material as if nothing significant has happened. After all, you have not yet received payment, so hold your celebration until your job is done.

If it is not only your job to sell your product but also to walk the customer through the closing paperwork, then please remember the **rule of simplicity.** Summarize the paperwork into normal conversation instead of reading it word for word. You are not a lawyer and you certainly do not want to act like one. *Translate*, if you will, the paperwork into everyday terms. Those of you who have ever closed on a house can recall the paperwork involved; it takes two hours just to glance at the papers! If you were to read each line, then your mind would wander and your logical mind would ponder whether you are making a good decision or not. Be silly, be natural, be confident, be simple. Speak in terms that someone at their laziest could understand. This is how you receive payment. This is how deals are done.

Chapter 5 / Priming

"Priming" is the art of inducing a certain behavior in someone by first exposing them to similar behaviors. The art of priming is subtle, simple, and powerful. Once understood and practiced, it can be put to use in many different ways. Life is a series of interactions with people and priming gives you an advantage in this multitude of interactions. In your case, the target behavior could be influencing the customer to hand you a credit card, or fill out some paperwork, or even just say the word 'yes.' Before explaining step-by-step how to do each of these things, first look at some joke-like examples of priming in order to get a clear picture of what priming actually is:

<u>Example 1</u>

"I met a girl the other day named Sally. She told me that her mom had five daughters and that she named them "Monday," "Tuesday," "Wednesday," "Thursday," and _____.

If your brain told you the next daughter was named "Friday," it is because you were primed to think so. Clearly, the fifth daughter's name is Sally!

Example 2

Question: What kind of tree does an acorn turn into?

Answer: Oak

Question: What are the wires in a bicycle wheel called?

Answer: Spokes

Question: What is the white of an egg called?

Answer: _____.

Although your guard is probably up now, you may still have considered the answer "yolk." Of course, the yolk is *not* the white of the egg.

It doesn't matter how smart you may or may not be. Following patterns is how everyone functions. If you see brake lights on the car in front of you, then you should slow down too. If you smell smoke, then you assume there is something burning. If you see a bloodthirsty bear in front of you, then you assume you are in danger. This is exactly what has given mankind the ability to survive for thousands of years! Everyone is a creature of habit, and following day to day patterns is done quite unconsciously. **Priming is simply beginning the target pattern and then letting the customer finish it.**

In the previous examples, priming was used to elicit a specific spoken word, "Friday" and "yolk." Let us instead prime the word '**yes**!' Salesmen have referred to yes-priming as "walking up a yes-ladder." If the customer says yes at least two times, they will certainly say it a third time. Try this by first asking the customer some obvious yes-questions and follow those with your target yes-question. As a simple example, imagine you are to close a customer with the line, "Do you want one?" Even though this closing line does not assume the "yes" or employ a choice close, it explains why risking a yes/no question as a closing line is much easier to do after priming the target answer. For example, you might ask the customer the following three questions after ending your pitch:

"...and if you get one today, they don't even charge for shipping."

"Does that make sense?"	[Customer: "Yes"]
"That's cool, right?"	[Customer: "Yes"]
"You want one?"	[Customer: "Yes!"]

Instead of closing using a yes/no question, a good salesperson will often prime the target 'yes' response but then either assume the close or offer a choice close. Example 3 shows an assumed close after yes-priming, and Example 4 shows a choice close after yes-priming:

Example 3

Salesperson: ...and if you pick it up today then it comes with this mount too. Does that make sense?

Customer: "Yeah."

Salesperson: "That's cool, right?"

Customer: "Yeah."

Salesperson: [scans item] Okay, your TV and your mount are waiting for you at checkout! Right this way!

Example 4

Salesperson: ...and if you pick it up today then it comes with this mount too. Does that make sense?

Customer: "Yeah."

Salesperson: "That's cool, right?"

Customer: "Yeah."

Salesperson: Would you like for us to deliver it, or would you rather take it home today?

It is most likely the case that you will be ending your pitch with choice closes instead of yes/no questions; however, priming can be even more subtle than the previous example. Climbing the yes-ladder so rapidly can appear obvious, even to the unsuspecting. How, then, can you more naturally put priming to use? It's simple: only ask yes-questions throughout your pitch.

How Deals Are Done

If you know the customer has two kids, you might say something along the lines of, "You have two kids, right?". The customer will answer "yes" and you move on. If you know the customer is looking for a truck, you may say something like, "...and that's why you want a truck, right?". Again, the customer says "yes" and you continue with your pitch. If your customer lives on a certain side of town you may say "Oh that's over there close to the [whatever landmark], right?". You get the idea. If you are going to risk your rhythm and put the ball in the customer's court, only do so if you can predict what the customer will do. If the customer is only allowed to say "yes" over and again, then they will be ripe for the closing in no time!

Priming is not limited to eliciting verbal responses – it can be used with actions as well. Now that you get the idea of how priming works, what about priming someone to fill out paperwork? Imagine you have a contract and a customer in front of you. It is now your goal to get the customer to complete that paperwork. Start by first writing something on the paperwork yourself. Monkey see monkey do. Next, ask (or tell) the customer to fill out something very easy, perhaps their name or the date. Gradually step up the responsibility of the items they are filling out. The further they go, the more obligated they will be to continue. As long as you maintain your rhythm and keep the paperwork summarized and simple, the customer will continue without hesitation.

Another common action in the field is asking for payment. The following suggestion should be used in almost every face-to-face transaction involving a target action of making payment with a debit or credit card. Since the target action involves pulling out a wallet and handing you a credit card, simply ask the customer to perform this exact action by first handing over a much less relevant card, such as, their identification. Once the customer reaches for their wallet, opens it, extracts their ID and hands it you, they are now much more likely to hand over the only card that matters to closing the deal. Once that ID hits your hand, do not skip a beat. Immediately ask for either their debit or credit card. Even if asking for cash, once the ID hits your hand it is immediately time to ask for payment.

Clearly, rhythm plays an internal role to every step of the sales process and it is probably most obvious when mastering priming. Attention to when and where to ask yes-questions will become part of your routine and will become second nature once you practice it thoroughly. When in the flow of your pitch, you will not want to be interrupted, you will not want the customer to take control. The customer may feel as though they are not involved if you are doing all of the talking, so give the customer an opportunity from time to time and let them answer 'yes' to a few questions during your routine. Once your routine is second nature and you've narrowed down some good yes-questions, it will seem as if the customer is just as much a part of the pitch as you are. In the same way that a juggler might ask a member of the audience to catch something and throw it back to him while maintaining his juggling routine, so can you perform your routine and trust the customer's involvement to only strengthen your pitch. Prime the "yes". Prime the pen. Prime the payment. This is how deals are done.

How Deals Are Done

Chapter 6 /
Overcoming Objections

If the answer is 'no' find out why. Then turn the why into a buy. Everything you have read up to this point is information that strengthens your routine. Practicing your routine to the point that it is completed without having to think about it should clearly be any salesperson's goal. Having a well-tuned routine will most certainly increase your confidence and increase your sales; however, the battle is rarely won by simply saying your lines. Undoubtedly, the customer will see the value in your product and will understand the benefits of buying, but often the customer will be reluctant to commit to buying right away. The real meat and potatoes of any great closer is measured by one's ability to handle objections.

First, allow yourself to consider the differences between **agreeing** with someone and **disagreeing** with someone. When agreeing with someone, both parties are marching in the same philosophical direction and everything is just hunky-dory. When disagreeing with someone, as if during a debate, it is rare that one party decides to change their views and march in the opposite direction. Why is that? Why is it the case that debates only further entrench the opposing parties in their opposing views?

Imagine an extreme example of something that is undeniably right or wrong, i.e. a math problem. If two people debate the value of 2+2 as either 4 or 5, obviously someone is right and someone else is wrong. If the debater on the side of arguing in favor of 4 shows the proof to the other debater, then they can literally prove themselves correct and their opponent incorrect. Now imagine 2 apples and 2 more apples are shown to the debater who argued 5 and he is proven wrong upon seeing only 4 apples. What we are left with is a person, now embarrassed and angered that they were wrong in the first place, and instead of saying, "By golly, I sure was wrong!" they instead say, "This is stupid! I'm out of here!"

Long story short, **seeking to prove people wrong only creates opponents.** It is the job of the salesperson to be a great **convincer**, a great **negotiator**. Seek not to be the smartest person in the land, seek to be the richest. How, then, can you convince people to see things your way if you are busy agreeing with them? There are two ways: (1) Verbal Kung Fu and (2) telling stories.

Verbal Kung Fu (VKF) is a comical name for a practical method of overcoming objections. VKF is a three-step process and is very simple to understand. Why Kung Fu? Instead of getting into a verbal boxing match and throwing punches at one another, it will be your goal to take the customer's energy and redirect it. Do not fight them; work with them.

The first step is simply agreeing with the customer. If the customer says they do not have any money for your product, tell them they are right. If the customer tells you they do not have the time to enjoy your product, do not correct them. If the customer tells you they simply have no need for what you are selling, act like you understand. What happens here is that you are avoiding being on the proverbial "opposite side of the table." Instead, you are presenting yourself as being on their side and understanding exactly how they are feeling. You do not want to enter a debate with the customer. If you do and you are proven right in the end, they will still feel as if you are wrong for pointing out their mistakes. Do not deny their perspective, just agree with it and then you can guide it in another direction.

Step two is turning their reason for objecting into their new reason for buying. There are likely many reasons why the customer is wrong about their objections; however, if you use their own reason for not buying and turn it into a reason for buying, then the customer might begin to see things from a new perspective. They won't be inclined to fight you about it either, because it is their own reason that is leading them back to the buy.

Step three is the simplest of all: go for the close again! Often, rookie salespeople follow the first two steps of agreeing and redirecting only to wait for the customer to beg for paperwork or something. That just won't happen!   After showing the customer why they should buy, now show them how to buy. Get the payment, get the yes, get the paperwork. Do not wait for the customer to admit how right you are. Just assume they understand and move back around to the close.

An example might sound something like this:

"Hey, I totally get it, you're on a budget. Which is exactly why you mentioned finding a TV under your price range. Would it be easier to pay cash or did you want to make payments?"

As you can see, there are only three lines here, one pertaining to each step of VKF. **Step one** is clearly agreeing that the customer does not have the money today. The customer wants a TV or they would not be looking. The only way to find out if they have the money or not is to ask for it, perhaps more than once. **Step two** is turning their excuse into the exact reason why they picked out that certain TV in the first place. Essentially, the tiedown holds them accountable here. **Step three** is just a simple question close. Either way, the only exit is by paying you for the TV.

If you are having trouble employing VKF in your duties as a salesperson, remember this line, **"That's exactly why…"**. Beginning your step-two is the only real challenge to VKF, but finding a way to guide their reasoning back to buying seems to come naturally if you just begin by saying, "That's exactly why…" The rest of the reasoning will flow right out. "Yeah, I totally see what you mean. That's exactly why…Would you like this one or that one?"

Verbal Kung Fu can be strengthened yet one step further by pouring more energy into one of the three steps described here. Take a moment to guess which step you think that is? Should you agree more? Should you redirect more? Should you close more? What would the results be?

The best results have been found in putting more energy into agreeing. There have been cases when simply feeding into the customer's reasoning shows them that you are so much on their side and the power is entirely theirs, that they decide to go ahead and close with you simply because you're such an understanding person. For example, someone might claim that they have no time for enjoying your product, so you simply get into the why of their having no free time. The customer says they work all the time and would not really be able to enjoy your product. You can then ask where they work and how long they've been there. You can get into how that person chose that type of work and all the mundane details they disclose. You simply ride the wave of their being so busy that they don't have time for your product. And then, you finally tell the customer that someone who works that hard certainly deserves a break. Thank God they met you! Now you can help them out and sell them your product! Eureka! They should have bought from you a year ago and they would have been much happier now!

Honestly, if enough time is spent dwelling on the first step of VKF (agreeing with the customer) then little effort is needed in doing steps two and three. The customer may close themselves since you are seemingly dropping the sale to sympathize with them.

Another great method for overcoming objections is that of **telling stories.** Storytelling and VKF are similar in that they share the three steps of agree / redirect / close; however, the main difference here is that, instead of redirecting the customer's original excuse, you simply put them in the shoes of someone else who was once in their position. Essentially, storytelling is a powerful step-two.

The power of storytelling is in the all-encompassing power of the imagination. When people hear stories, they place themselves in the shoes of the characters in the stories. That is the reason stories are interesting in the first place! Words have the power of capturing the imagination, so by telling someone a story, they cannot help but listen. If a customer pushes back on your close by saying that they simply do not have the money today, a wise salesperson might do the following: first agree, then tell a story of someone in a similar position who decided to actually buy, and then go for the close. It might sound something like this:

"Yeah, this is a pretty expensive TV. You know, I talked to a guy last week about this TV and he came in this store four times and looked at this TV before he ever bought it. He didn't want to pay that much either, but he finally decided that it was an inevitable purchase since TVs just keep getting better and better. Sooner or later he would have spent so much time looking at different TVs and prices that it made more sense to just buy the TV he knew he wanted. After all, it's not like it breaks the bank or anything. I mean, you get what you pay for, and in the long run he got what he wanted and he could not have been any more pleased. I mean, why read the menu when you know you want a steak, right?"

When you share your experiences with the customer, they re-live those experiences for themselves. By telling them stories of people in similar positions, you allow them to travel through time and absorb someone else's experience. Also, the pressure is off of the customer since you are not directly convincing them to go ahead and make the purchase. Helping the customer to see things in a new light is the whole point to overcoming objections and storytelling is an undeniably strong way of accomplishing this goal.

When deciding what stories to tell, only choose stories that are true! Take the time to consider the common objections in your field and find stories that relate to each of the situations. If you can't think of a story pertaining to these situations then find one that pertains to a colleague. There is no shame in telling someone else's story as long as you are telling it truthfully. For instance, do not tell a story about your cousin as if it's a story about you. Stick to the truth and your story will be much more convincing. People may not know for certain when they are being lied to, but they can feel it. Telling untruthful stories will only hurt you in the long run. The truth, after all, is what will be convincing to the customer. Dodging the truth would only be dodging the close. The method is simply to understand the customer's common objections and relate them to stories that you know. Do the research and think of some good stories already! What are you waiting for?

Finally, a how-to guide for sales tactics would be incomplete without addressing the notorious objection of "I'll think about it". It does not matter what line of sales you work in, you will often hear this deflection. Dealing with objections can be very straight forward, but how do you deal with an objection that does not have an identifiable argument? How do you agree, flip, and close an objection that is open ended? Easy! **Just ask the customer for help!**

Verbal Kung Fu is simple once you have something tangible, so simply ask the customer what is holding them back? What exactly do they have to think about? Once they cough up an excuse, you can apply the rules of VKF and turn them back into buying reasons. If the customer seems reluctant to offer anything tangible, give them some choices. Remember, you are helping the customer come to the conclusion of buying, so help them through this roadblock as well.

Take this exchange for example:

Customer: "I don't know, I'll have to think about it."

Salesperson: "Hey, that's normal, you want to think it over. I'm curious, what's holding you back?"

At this point, the customer may offer a tangible excuse. If the customer says the money or the shipping or the timing is not to their liking, then you have something with which to apply your VKF; however, they may also keep delaying the close…

Customer: "Oh, I don't know, I just have a lot to think about."

Salesperson: "Hey, that's fine. I mean, you like the TV you picked out, right? [yes] And you found something under your price range, right? [well, yeah]

Okay, then would you be more comfortable making low monthly payments or would you rather just get a discount today for paying in cash?"

A **story** version of overcoming this objection can also be used:

Customer: "Oh, I don't know, I just have a lot to think about."

Salesperson: "Hey, that's fine, there's a lot of different TVs out there and a lot of different deals to get. I remember the time my dad went looking for a TV for his man-cave. He found a good one, but he was worried about spending that much. He put off buying it so long that the discounts they offered him expired and he ended up getting something else. I mean, he still ended up getting a TV, it just wasn't the perfect match. I know you're hesitant to get this one, and that's fine. If you want to get it today, though, then we can possibly do no payments for the first two months."

It is important to note that no matter what tactic you employ to overcome the customer's objections, be aware of the word **"but"**. Avoid it at all costs! Whenever someone says "but" they are contradicting the first half of their point with their second half. Notice the drastic difference between these two seemingly similar statements:

1. "I understand it's expensive, **but** you said it's in your price range, right?"

2. "I understand it's expensive, **and** you said it's in your price range, right?"

The first of the two sentences calls the customer out to explain himself. In short, you are on your way to beginning an argument. You have shown the customer that he is contradicting himself and has some explaining to do. No matter if you are right or wrong about the situation, the customer will not feel good about buying once you have proven yourself correct. Sentence number two, on the other hand, shows a helping hand. By simply changing the word "but" to "and", you show the customer that you, too, are interested in finding a good fit for them. From this point, the customer must choose to either stay in that price range or pick a new one. Both of those choices still end with you getting paid. Although this point is hardly touched upon in this book, it can be a very powerful tool. The reader is encouraged to examine their own habits and routines and rid themselves of the word "but". Just swap **"but"** with the word **"and"**!

"Obviously, you want to strengthen your selling skills, **but** will you actually put these suggestions to use?"

Versus…

"Obviously, you want to strengthen your selling skills, **and** you will actually put these suggestions to use, right?"

In summary, Verbal Kung Fu is a three-step process: **agree / redirect / close**. If more time is to be spent on any of these three steps, invest time in agreeing. The more you ask the customer about their excuse, the better you can help them get what you both want. Pour your efforts into helping the customer get what they want and they will be more inclined to agree to buy. A parallel tactic to VKF is **storytelling**. Find examples of people similar to your customers so you can share their experiences with them. If the customer can begin to identify with someone who has already weathered the storm (and decided to buy) then they are one step closer to paying you. This is how 'no's become 'yes's. This is how deals are done.

Chapter 7 / Accountability

Holding yourself accountable for your own actions is how you grow. If you want to get better at any skill then keeping track of your failures and your victories allows you to see what works and what does not work. Clearly, if you are reading this book on how to sell, you desire your skills to grow. Reading this book is a good place to start gathering new ideas to grow your skills. Actually practicing these ideas – not just one or two of them but all of them – is the next step to growing your skills. Finally, keeping track of your actions will allow you to look back on everything you have done that day and reflect on your progress. In order to hold yourself accountable, there is a simple tool you can use called a **Daily Action Report, or DAR**.

Creating a Daily Action Report is simple. Find a piece of paper and write out how many pitches you are going to do for the day/week/month depending on what it is you sell and/or how often you actually perform your routine. If, for example, you are selling TVs and you might approach five customers an hour for eight hours, then your DAR should have the numbers 1 through 40 on it. The simplest way to use the DAR is after every pitch you write either a √ or an X depending on whether you closed the customer or not.

Keep this piece of paper in your pocket and update it after every pitch. If you are brand new to the world of sales, then perhaps writing a √ or an X would be more appropriate to whether or not you felt good about your pitch with each customer. However, after a month or so you will feel comfortable with your routine and you should use the DAR to keep track of your sales.

There are many benefits to using a Daily Action Report. First, creating a list of the number of pitches you expect to get in a day/week/month is essentially the act of putting your goals on paper. Once you see the goals you have set for yourself, you can now easily act upon them. Once you write the numbers 1 through 40 on your DAR, the clock begins to tick and it is time to start holding yourself accountable for the work you will do. The first thing you will notice is how many pitches you typically can perform within one hour. If you pitch more than five times in one hour then clearly you will need more numbers on your DAR. If you pitch less than five times per hour then either you need less numbers on your DAR or you need to find a way to make more pitches.

The next thing you will notice about yourself is how many pitches you normally require in order to get a sale. If you usually see eight X's before you see one √ then you are only closing one out of nine pitches. Whether or not that is considered a good thing will be determined by the products you are selling. However, the real question is whether or not that is where you want to be with your ability to close sales! Challenge yourself to become a stronger closer, and you will notice your DAR begin to represent the same. Soon there will be five X's for every √. Now you are closing one out of six pitches. Not long thereafter you should begin to see two X's for every √, meaning you are reliably closing one out of three pitches! As long as you are focused on growing your skill and growing your paycheck, you will be rewarded by keeping track of your pitches with a DAR.

There are other helpful things to note when using a DAR besides just pitches and closes. Instead of writing X's after each pitch you did not close, you could instead write exactly the objection the customer used in order to dodge the sale. At first, you may notice a myriad of excuses. However, after a while, you may begin to see a pattern of one or two certain objections that you usually cannot overcome. What a good teacher you can be to yourself! If your DAR shows that you are usually held back by customers with the same excuses, then you know exactly what kind of advice and training to seek next in order to further your skills. In this sense, the DAR can serve as a way of spotlighting your weaknesses, therefore allowing you to finely tune your skills as a salesperson.

Also, facing rejection over and over again can be the thread that unravels any salesperson. If pulled too often, soon there will be nothing left but a sour, de-

feated salesperson. Dealing with rejection is yet another strength of using a DAR, because it relieves you
of the burden of carrying each "no" on your shoulder.
Think about it – would you rather be told "no" an
innumerable amount of times or would you rather
count the number of "no's" it takes to get to the next
predictable "yes". In this sense, knowing that you require four X's on average before you can achieve one
$\sqrt{}$, means that the X's are just stepping-stones to your
next "yes". They are just a part of the landscape of
finding your next deal. They are just the number of
times you must cast your line before you can finally
catch a nice juicy fish. If you have not closed a deal in
a while and are pitching under average for yourself,
then rest assured that your next pitch will surely close.
You have the proof right there in front of you!

Make a game of using your DAR. Once you become familiar with your ability to close deals, you can
then begin to challenge yourself accordingly. If you
are used to closing four deals a day/week/month, then
it is time to up your skills once again and aim to close
one more. Remember to be proud of your accom-
plishments! What is the point of holding yourself
accountable if you cannot reward yourself once in a
while? Obviously, your paychecks will serve as a re-
minder of your progress, but you may not see them
immediately. Your DARs, however, will be your mo-
mentary trophies. Perhaps you should frame some of
your most memorable DARs! Learning from your

defeats and celebrating your victories are the only real ways to learn anything at all, so help yourself out and carry a DAR for every shift. Create this simple and profitable habit. This is how progress is made. This is how deals are done.

How Deals Are Done

Chapter 8 / Attitude

There exists a saying, "Sales is 10% technique and 90% attitude." Nothing could be closer to the truth. Everything you have read up to this point has been about technique. Although technique is still necessary in order to complete a sale, it would not find any traction without the right **attitude** to deliver it. A rookie salesperson who wants the sale more than a veteran wants it is more likely to close, because it is he/she that the customer will be drawn to. People do business with people. Imagine for a moment that you have been rejected several times over the last four hours. How will that affect your attitude? How will that affect your next pitch? The only way to be graceful with rejection and make your twenty-first pitch seem as if it is your very first pitch is to get out there and test yourself. It is much easier to read these words than it is to live them, but please remember that **your attitude is completely your choice.**

Every salesperson faces rejection. Such is the nature of the job. Just remember that the road to "yes" is paved with "no's". Clues have been left throughout this book that tip your attitude in the right direction. Many of the previous chapters allude toward obtaining that positive attitude every salesperson needs. For instance, if you are a card-carrying DAR user, then you will have the advantage of collecting "no's" and converting them into stepping stones that lead toward a "yes". Priming the "yes" also primes you, the salesperson, for expecting the "yes" once it is time to close. Also, the warm-up allows you and the customer to both relax and focus on topics other than sales, thereby cultivating the right emotional attitudes.

How then can you work on improving your attitude? Start by being aware of your thoughts and words. **Your thoughts turn into words and your words turn into reality.** Please take a moment to understand the profound truth of the previous sentence. Here it is once more: your thoughts turn into words and your words turn into reality. This is a double-edged sword! If you say you are weak, then you are weak. If you say you are strong, then you are strong! If you say you will not close any deals, then you won't. If you say you are going to set record sales, then you just might actually accomplish a new record. The truth could not be simpler! This is the power of intention and imagination. If your thoughts are dominated by negativity, you will create a negative outcome. If your thoughts are dominated by a positive, adaptable attitude, then you will learn and grow and find deals by the end of the day.

Once you are taking account of your thoughts, be careful what you choose to say out loud. When your grandmother said "Be careful what you wish for, you just might get it" she was absolutely right. Your own words can serve as a feedback loop. If you are feeling on edge and your attitude could tip in either direction, what words would guide you back toward staying positive and what words would have the opposite effect? If you lose a sale and say "That was total B.S! That idiot should've just handed me his credit card. I can't believe I wasted my time with that jerk!", what effect do you think that will have on your attitude? Alternatively, if you lose a sale and say "The road to "yes" is paved with "no's". Some will, some won't, so what, next!", what effect will *that* choice have on your attitude? Your thoughts and words shape your entire day. The result is your choice.

Sometimes, the difficulty lies in believing your own words. An easy remedy for this is just to repeat the words over and over. You might not believe yourself the first time you say the words out loud, but you definitely will by the twentieth or even the fiftieth time. Try telling yourself, "Today is the best day ever." Upon uttering it once, it may seem corny. Say it one hundred times and you just might start to believe it as fact. Once you believe it, you are certain to have the advantageous attitude necessary for closing your target amount of deals. Speak into existence that which you desire!

Finally, a well accomplished salesperson is a **confident** salesperson. Confidence comes from two major places: (1) your previous success in doing the very job you are doing now, and (2) the healthiness of your life in general. Speaking to the latter, it is hard to be confident when you have marital issues, drug addictions, chronic tardiness, or a terrible diet. Getting your life in order is a major part of being a confident person in all aspects of life. After all, if you cannot take care of yourself, how can you take care of your job? How to get your life in order is not the aim of this book; however, it is worth noting that a healthy life leads to confidence and confidence leads to more income. The former source for confidence is much easier to tackle in a how-to book such as this one. In short, successful selling leads to more successful selling and so on. If you are reading this book, then you have either been unsuccessful in sales up to this point or you are simply looking to up your sales game. If that is the case, then practice this confidence-building exercise before the beginning of each of your shifts.

The exercise is known as **One Minute Expert** (OME). OME is not only a fun game to play before your shifts, but it is also a fun game to play at parties! The rules are very simple: pretend as if you are the local expert on any given topic for at least one full minute. First, the group chooses a random topic, for example, tigers. Then, someone introduces the first player as if they are interviewing them. It might sound something like this,

"And here we are at the ballpark with our local expert on tigers, Steve Long."

How Deals Are Done

Once Steve is handed the pretend microphone, their one-minute time limit begins. For that full minute, Steve must shine with so much confidence while describing whatever he can think of about the random topic of tigers that he appears to truly be the local expert on that topic. In this example, whether or not Steve knows anything about tigers, he has one minute to *pretend* like he does! OME is truly a lot of fun and can really boost your confidence before a shift. How does it do that, you might ask? If you can challenge yourself to appear confident while describing topics unknown to you, then it is quite easy to appear confident by the time you are actually working and performing your usual routine. It is as if you are lifting 50 pounds in preparation for lifting five pounds.

Naturally, a positive and confident salesperson will have the most advantageous attitude for sales. The customer, too, wants to be positive and confident in their buying decision, so show them what that looks like. You will find that the more fun you are having, the more deals you will close. And the more deals you close will lead to more fun that you are having.

Be positive. Be confident. This is how deals are done.

How Deals Are Done

Chapter 9 / Goals

Successful people know what it is that they want, so it is time to define your goals if you are going to successfully chase them. Try hitting a bullseye without seeing a target. Where do you even aim? Think about your goals as if they are a treasure map, because, essentially, they are. Where do you begin and where do you end? What does success even look like? What would be considered a victory? You are encouraged to think big! Give yourself a reputation to live up to! Speak into existence the new version of yourself by setting benchmarks along the path to becoming a greater person. Practicing goal-setting is beneficial in all parts of your life, but this book will simply cover goal-setting that is relevant to sales.

Imagine your typical shift, goal-less and mundane. You show up, clock in, and start pitching people. Maybe you will close some deals. Maybe you won't. But at least you are working, right? The shift ends and you closed an uneventful amount of sales. You get to keep your job, but no one is impressed, especially not your paycheck. You start to think about getting another sales job. "Maybe I could close twice as many deals over there." But once the grass-is-greener mentality wears off, you will just be right back where you started – bored and not much to show for it. You continue on day-to-day without a challenge and without the rush that sales used to bring you daily. Chances are that if you are reading this book, then you are already tired of this vicious cycle. Time to break out of it!

Three types of goals will be described here: **pre-shift goals, shift goals,** and **long-term goals.** Each of these goals work together in order to create the momentum you are looking for. Building up momentum streamlines success in your life. The same can be said about failure after failure. Think about your life as a giant metal ball. The more momentum it has, the easier it is to keep it rolling in the right direction. If the ball is moving slowly or just sitting there going nowhere, then getting the ball to move is going to require a good amount of work. Get started and get pushing, but do not give up! Set some goals for yourself, keep pushing, and give that ball the momentum it needs!

First things first, set a goal for yourself to accomplish before you even begin your shift. Think about it – what is something simple that you could do before your next shift that would help you become the salesperson that you want to become? Try some of these suggestions: listen to a motivational song, watch a motivational video, eat a meal, do 50 jumping-jacks, recite a poem, call your spouse, practice your pitch, read a chapter in this book, etc. The point is that you begin your shift with a small victory. That way, you can ride the feeling of victory into your shift in order to create victory where it really counts. Every salesperson knows that the best time to sell is right after you sell. In other words, victory follows victory. Knowing this, wouldn't it be wise to celebrate a small victory before you even clock in? Of course it would!

The strongest pre-shift goal you can do is **visualization**. When you show up to work, stay in the car and turn off your radio. Imagine yourself clocking in and saying hi to your co-workers. Imagine yourself creating a DAR with your target amount of pitches for the day, pitching and pitching and pitching, and maintaining a great attitude. Now imagine yourself overcoming multiple objections and actually hitting your desired number of closes. Once you have taken the time to see what it is that you want, now it is time to go and live it. A target you have seen is a target that is easy to hit. Sometimes you have to see it in order to believe it. Take the time to *see* it with your visualization.

Next, set a goal to hit during your shift. Maybe you tell yourself that your goal is closing four deals. Or perhaps you would rather simply set a goal for the number of pitches you need for the entire shift. Maybe you just set a goal of improving your closing ratio. Whatever the case may be, give yourself a goal for each shift. It is important that you reflect on your goal as well. Do not ask something of yourself that is too outrageous to accomplish. Likewise, do not give yourself a goal that is so mediocre that you will obviously attain it. If you are hitting your goals during your shift and still have time left on the clock, do not kick your feet up! Keep going!

Pre-shift goals and shift goals are important short-range goals, but please do not neglect to set long term goals as well. How much money are you wanting to make this year? If you do not have an answer to that question already then decide that amount right now before reading any further. Done? Okay. Now break that amount down into a month and then a week and then day and then an hour until you finally know what is necessary of yourself in order to achieve the income you desire. The beauty of commission jobs is that you can literally choose your income and go out there and do something about it. You are in charge of your goals; therefore, you are in charge of your income.

Another step in the right direction for goal-setting is monitoring how you talk about your goals: what words do you use to describe them? When speaking about your goals, do not *hope* that you will hit them. Do not *try* to attain your goals. Strike those two words out of your vocabulary completely, because they are useless to successful salesmen. If you truly believe that you will reach your sales goals, then speak about them as if they are certain to happen. Tell yourself, "I am closing four deals today for sure!" Another word to strike out of your vocab is "can't." What-you-can't-do does not get you paid. Focus on what-you-can-do and keep improving from there. Instead of telling yourself "I can't close that many deals" say something along the lines of "I haven't closed that many deals *yet*." Think of it like learning any other skill. To say that you cannot play the violin is just plain nonsense as long as you still have two hands! The *truth* is that you just have not learned to play the violin *yet*. Simple changes in your language can have profound effects on your life and on your paycheck.

There is one more landmine to be avoided when considering how you speak about your goals. Be careful of justifying your defeats by saying "I'll make up for it tomorrow". If you have tried your best all day and finally after your shift you say "I'll make up for it tomorrow", then, yes, you are assuredly being positive. If you are only half way through your shift and you say "It's okay, I'll make up for it tomorrow", then, no, you are not being positive, and you are not speaking into existence the attainment of your goals. Procrastination does not attain anything. Laziness will not get you paid. There is no good replacement for hard work, so set your goals and stick to them the very best that you can.

Keep track of your ability to reach your goals. Own up to your successes and also your failures. As your skills grow, so should your goals. Challenge yourself and do not give in to negligence. Only you set your own horizons and only you will tell yourself what you can and cannot do. Never stop creating bigger and better treasure maps.   This is how you get what you want. This is how deals are done.

Chapter 10 / Honesty

Learn how to deliver the truth and you will learn how to sell. Everyone has heard the cliché of the liar salesperson; he will say anything to close a deal. For most people, conjuring up the idea of a salesperson is identical to that of picturing a liar. If mere words stood between you and a bigger paycheck, then wouldn't the average person simply say what is necessary in order to get paid? Well, yes and no. Although it is true that there are liars within the sales profession, it is likewise true that there are liars in any profession. The fact of the matter is that customers will *expect* a salesperson to say whatever is necessary in order to close a deal. Knowing this fact can be used to your advantage in a big way.

Essentially, the art of designing a pitch lies in strategic presentation, but since the customer fully expects you to only tell them the good aspects of what they are buying, try including some truthful, less tasteful details as well. Showing the customer that what they are buying is a real-world product and is not a godsend fairy-tale product lets the customer feel as if they are being shown the full array of points necessary to make a wise buying decision. Chances are, the customer already knows something about the product you are pitching, so coming out with the good and the bad, before the customer can identify it themselves, takes away their ammo once it is time for objections. Doing this not only makes the product seem more realistic, but it also makes you seem more like a person that truly wants to help the customer get what they want.

A good way to deliver such information is by using an old teachers' technique called **"the sandwich"**. The idea is simple: good information + target information + good information. Examples may sound something like this:

- "This TV is 60 inches, and is a bit expensive, and it can link with your phone."

- "This car is the color you want, it doesn't have a warranty, and it does come with airbags liked you asked."

- "We'll cover the cost of the room, you cover the taxes, and we'll include the waterpark passes as well."

As you can see, weaving the information between good and bad lets all of it sink in without leaving a bad taste in the customer's mouth. The good information serves as bookends for the less tasteful parts included in the middle. Taking a big bite out of this delivery not only leaves the customer with well-rounded knowledge of your product but it also tends to build trust in the salesperson as a helpful guide in making their buying decisions.

Similar to the idea of the sandwich is that of the **"takeaway."** A book on sales would be incomplete without the mention of the takeaway. The sandwich is a technique for delivering information that either must be included in your pitch or information that helps to rebalance your product's believability. But the takeaway, on the other hand, leaves the customer with only a taste of what they want and then removes their beloved new product from them.

Timing, as in all things, can make or break the delivery of a takeaway. Only use this technique when you know the customer is on board to buy but simply does not agree to the terms. Perhaps meeting all of the customer's demands takes away from your possible commission. Perhaps the longer the customer takes, the more time you are missing with other customers. Perhaps the more perks you include, the less believable your product becomes and the more desperate you seem. If any of these situations is recognizable, then it is time to use the takeaway. Just draw a line in the sand and apologize to the customer that the product you have simply cannot satisfy all of their needs. Once the customer feels the emptiness of loss, they should take a step closer toward accepting your terms for the sale. The idea is that the customer is **pulled** toward your product instead of having it **pushed** on them. Doing this runs the risk of letting the customer walk away, but after all, you only use the takeaway when you are nearing a loss. This show of truthfulness defines the boundaries for the negotiation and gets you closer to closing.

Keep in mind that the temptation to close a deal by lying is a shortcut that will only set you back in the long run. If you give in to dishonesty to make more money then you will also give up on your efforts to grow your skills as a professional salesperson. A choice must be made. If you've made the wrong choice in the past, then the opportunity remains to come back to the more powerful, truthful side of sales. Remember, everyone has an ability to detect BS. Maybe they cannot put it into words, but they can definitely sense it. The customer may even ask you leading questions just to determine if you would represent your product untruthfully. By presenting the customer with the truthfully lackluster details as well as the attractive details do you then present yourself as a helpful informer as opposed to a simple salesperson, out to find an extra dollar. Long story short, telling the truth in a strategic, professional manner is the only way to mastering sales. The truth will always benefit you. Learn how to deliver the truth and you will learn how to sell. This is how deals are done.

A Final Word

Sales is an interesting profession. No matter your upbringing, no matter your level of education, no matter your age, the playing field is level. Becoming successful in sales comes down to personal drive. How strongly do you want to grow? How ready are you to accept your failures along with your victories? How much about yourself are you willing to learn?

The sales profession can be a great personal teacher. There are people of all income levels in the exact same position, so ask yourself "Why is it that person-A makes $120,000 and I only make $40,000?". Essentially, you have the same job as they do, so realize the fact that you have some room to grow. As you learn more and more about yourself, you may not like what you find. Facing your roadblocks is a part of personal growth and can be painful. Rest assured that this process of pain and growth will never end unless, of course, you would rather just keep making mediocre paychecks. Do not criticize the successful people around you. Instead, compliment them! Why spit on a Ferrari when you could drive one?

No matter your motivation for reading this book, know that you can make a change in your paycheck and even your personal life by taking advice. Do not neglect the advice of teachers. Do not pick and choose which advice you take and which you will not. Practice every suggestion in this book! How else could you determine its worth? You will find that you are your own best teacher. Only you know what it is that you lack and only you can motivate yourself to get up and do something about it. Walk the walk of your predecessors and then become curious for more. Perfect every suggestion in this book and then write your own book full of closing tools for the next generation to perfect. Get out there and show us how deals are done.

How Deals Are Done